LIVE BY FAITH

Stephen Kaung

ISBN: 978-1-942521-01-3

Available from:

Christian Testimony Ministry
4424 Huguenot Road
Richmond, Virginia 23235

www.christiantestimonyministry.com

Printed in USA

CONTENTS

Stephen Kaung spoke the messages contained in this booklet at the Northeast Christian weekend conference in Long Beach Island, New Jersey in October 2013. The spoken words have been transcribed by permission with only minimal editing for clarity. Unless otherwise indicated, Scripture quotations are from the New Translation by J. N. Darby.

1. THE COMMENCEMENT OF FAITH

Hebrews 10:37-39, 11:1, 6—For yet a very little while he that comes will come, and will not delay. But the just shall live by faith; and, if he draw back, my soul does not take pleasure in him. But we are not drawers back to perdition, but of faith to saving [the] soul...Now faith is [the] substantiating of things hoped for, [the] conviction of things not seen...But without faith [it is] impossible to please [him]. For he that draws near to God must believe that he is, and [that] he is a rewarder of them who seek him out.

May we have a word of prayer:

Dear Lord, we want to thank Thee because of Thy precious promise that where two or three are gathered together unto My name, there am I in the midst of them. Lord, how we praise and thank Thee that Thou art here in our midst. Thou art our Lord, and we do come before Thy presence to worship Thee, to open our hearts to Thee, and to hear what Thou wants to say to us. Dear Lord, speak; Thy servants heareth. In Thy precious name. Amen.

We thank God for gathering us again unto Himself. I often feel that every time God's people are gathered together, it shows the mercy of God. He knows what we need, and He is ever ready to supply the need. So may the Lord be glorified in our midst.

I believe everybody knows the theme of this conference is: Live by Faith. The Scripture verses that are being used for this conference come from Hebrews 10:37-39, and they are wonderful verses.

A VERY LITTLE WHILE

"For yet a very little while." I was impressed with the words *very little while*. He that comes will come and will not delay. It has been more than two thousand years since our Lord promised that He will come back to receive us to Himself. Yet here it says, "for yet a very little while He will come and will not delay." A day is as a thousand years to the Lord, and a thousand years is as a day. In other words, it is only two days since He said these words—*a very little while*. So here we are after two thousand years, but so far as God is concerned, it is just two days. In Hosea it says, "on the third day he will raise us up" (6:2). Therefore, we are very, very close to the coming of the Lord. If the Lord should come now, how glorious it will be! And it is true, He can come at any moment.

We do realize as we approach the coming of the Lord, the days are getting more and more difficult. The enemy cannot do anything to the Lord; the only thing he can do to prevent the Lord's purpose being fulfilled is to work against God's people. That is why as the coming of the Lord approaches, so far as we are concerned, the days get more and more difficult. But thank God, He has given us a secret. How can we endure these difficult times? It is by faith.

LIVING BY FAITH OR BY SELF

"But the just shall live by faith; and, if he draw back, my soul does not take pleasure in him" (v. 38). The Lord expects us to live by faith.

Oftentimes, when we think of this word "live by faith" our impression is that there are a few people who live by faith, which means they do no work and they live by trusting the Lord to supply their needs. That is their conception of living by faith; but that is not the Scriptural interpretation. By the grace of God every believer lives by faith. If you are not living by faith, what are you living by? You are living by your self and not trusting the Lord for your life. So we are not to be drawers back to perdition. To understand what this word *perdition* means you have to read the context. The book of Hebrews is written to believers; therefore, it does not refer to eternal death. Within the context of the book of Hebrews, perdition means you are not able to reign with Christ for a thousand years. Thank God, if we live by faith, then we are not drawers back to perdition, but by faith to the saving of the soul.

WHAT IS FAITH?

My assignment is the consummation of faith. But unless we know the commencement of faith, how can we talk about consummation? So I will go back to the very beginning.

What is faith? Hebrews 11:1 is the only place where faith is given some explanation. You cannot say it is the definition but at least it gives us some explanation. "Faith is the substantiating of things hoped for, the conviction of things not seen." This is the Darby version, and he tries to be very accurate to the original. Even though his English is not very smooth, it is very correct. So faith is the substantiating of things hoped for, the conviction of things not seen. When we are talking about faith, there are actually two things involved: the objective and the subjective. Faith has both its objective side and subjective side.

THE OBJECTIVE SIDE OF FAITH

The objective side is something outside of us, which means it is God. In Hebrews 11:6 it says, "Without faith it is impossible to please Him. For he that draws near to God must believe that He is, and that He is a rewarder of them who seek Him out." So first of all we need to know the objective side of faith. What is faith based upon? It tells us that the objective or the substance is

God. He is not only the substance of our faith, but He is a rewarder of them who seek Him out by faith. Therefore, the objective side of faith is God Himself. Thank God He *is*. He is the great I AM. In other words, He is everything to us. This is our God. Not only that, He is also a rewarder of those who seek after Him. In other words, if you seek after Him, He will reward you—even with Himself. That is the objective side of faith, and that is the substance. Darby uses the word substantiating here which is a verbal noun. The substance is there and we have the ability to bring that substance from outside into our inward experience. That is substantiating.

Let's take for instance this picture of the building that is on the wall where we are gathered. It is here; so that is the substance. Even before we came into the hall, it was already here. It does not depend upon our entrance into the building; it is already here. As we come into the building and look toward the front, we see the picture. But if a blind man comes into the building and we tell him there is a picture of the building on the wall, he will say, "I do not see it." Therefore, to him it is nothing; there is no substance there. Even though the substance is there, he cannot substantiate it, so he does not see it. Therefore, because he does not see it, to him this picture of the building is not there.

That is exactly what faith is. Faith is the substantiating of things hoped for and the conviction of things not seen. So far as truth is concerned, it is already there, and it is forever true. It never changes. Even if we do not see it, it does not disappear. Whether we see it or not it is there; it is an eternal fact. God *is*. He is the great I AM. He is everything we need. He is the first and the last, the eternal One. This is truth that is forever there whether we believe or not. But if we believe, we experience the glory of it.

Let's consider the rising of the sun. It so happened that before we came to the conference we stayed at a house where we could see the sun rise in the morning, and how beautiful it was! However, if I were blind, even if the sun rose in such a wonderful way, to me it would be nothing. But because it is nothing to me I cannot say there is no sunrise or that it will not rise because I do not see it. Whether we see it or not, it rises and it is so glorious. Blessed are those who can see the sun rise and can enjoy it. It is as if the sun rises in our heart and becomes our experience.

This is what faith is. There is no problem with the objective side because we are told in Hebrews 11:6 that God *is*, and He is the rewarder of those who seek after Him. This is eternal truth and never changes. The problem is with us— whether we believe it or not. If you believe it, you see it, and you have substantiated it. You begin to experience it, and it is wonderful. But if you do not have faith, it is like the blind who cannot see; to him there is nothing. So this is how important faith is.

Faith is like casting an anchor from the ship to steady it. Of course, you do not cast it on board but out to sea. You cast it into a place that you cannot see, but you know it will steady the ship. So faith is casting our anchor upon God who is and is the rewarder of all who seek Him.

FAITH IS LIVING

Now faith is a living thing. You remember in Luke 17 the Lord said: "If your brother sins against you and he comes to you and confesses his sin and asks your forgiveness, you forgive him even if he offended you seven times" (see vv. 3-4). But every time he comes back and says, "Excuse me," will you excuse him? When the disciples heard that, they said they could not do it. If a person sins against me one time, I suffer for it; the second time it becomes more difficult, but how can I forgive someone who sins against me seven times? It shows that he is not repentant at all; I cannot forgive him. The disciples were surprised and said: "Lord give us more faith." We have faith to forgive people once, but we do not have faith to forgive them seven times within a day. That is too much for us. However, the Lord said, "If your faith is like a mustard seed, you can command a sycamore tree to be planted in the sea" (see vv. 5-6). Now a mustard seed is the smallest of all seeds, but it is living; it has a life in it. Even though it is the smallest of all seeds, yet the Lord said, "If you have faith like a mustard seed, you can command the tree to be planted in the sea." That is impossible! How can a tree be planted in the sea? The Lord said, "Faith can do the impossible." That is what the Lord is expecting of each one of us. Do you really believe God? Do you really believe that He is, that He is everything to you? Do you believe that if you seek Him, He will reward you? If you do, that is living faith.

HOW TO OBTAIN LIVING FAITH

How can we get living faith? You cannot get it by turning to yourself. Somehow we tend to look within ourselves to see if there is faith there. But when we do this, we will never find faith there— only unbelief. Have you experienced that? I have. But if we want to truly have living faith, we have to look outside ourselves and look up to Jesus, the Author and Finisher of faith. He is the one who gives us faith, and He is the one who will complete our faith. Do not look at yourself. Do not look around you. Do not look at your brothers and sisters. The more you look at yourself, the more disappointed you are which results in despair. The more you look at your brothers and sisters, the more you also despair. But if we look away from these things and look to Jesus, He is the Author and Finisher of faith. This is actually what faith is.

LIVING FAITH WILL GROW

If faith is living it will grow, for everything that is living grows. If it does not grow, it shows there is no life. If there is life, it is bound to grow. We are born with a human life, and with this life, we grow from babyhood to childhood, from childhood to adolescence, from adolescence to adulthood. In other words, we have to grow up because there is life there. And it is the same thing with faith. If the faith is real, it is bound to grow. How will our faith grow? In His wonderful wisdom God shows us that the way of growth is by trials. If your faith is never tried, tested, or challenged your faith will never grow. And trials come from two directions. As we read the Bible, we find that trials may come from God Himself. He will test us. But they also may come from the enemy who will tempt us.

THE TRYING OF OUR FAITH: ABRAHAM

There is a great difference between testing and tempting. James tells us in his epistle that God never tempts anyone. He cannot be tempted and He will not tempt anyone. Temptation comes from the enemy. When God tests us or tries us, it is not temptation; it is testing. What is the difference? When God is testing us, He has already built faith in us. He will not test us beyond what He has put within us.

When God called Abraham out of Ur of the Chaldeans, he was to leave his family and his native home and go to where God would lead him. Abraham obeyed, but only partially, because he consulted with his father Terah. When his father realized that his son was determined to leave, he said he would leave with Abraham. In other words, the father took the lead. They left Ur of the Chaldeans and came to Haran, and the father said: "This is far enough; let us stay." When Abraham started this path of faith, he only succeeded halfway. We do not know how long Terah lived in Haran, but as long as he lived there with Abraham, there was no more revelation from above. It was not until God took Terah away that He said, "Go out from your kindred." But unfortunately, he took Lot with him. So in the beginning we find Abraham's faith was not perfect. But God knows, and He allows us to begin with imperfection. Now if you say, "Wait until I have faith then I will leave," you will stay in Ur of the Chaldeans. Go as far as you are able.

Abraham went to Canaan and there God tested him. While he was there, there was a famine, and without consulting God, Abraham went to Egypt. He tried to save the situation but he made it worse and he was stuck there. What could he do? Only God could intervene, and thank God, He did and delivered Abraham. Then he went back and built an altar to God.

Unfortunately Lot, his kindred, was with him, and they finally had to separate. Again God spoke to him. After Abraham saved Lot from the four kings, he got a great victory. However, we know that oftentimes after a great victory, a big letdown follows. It is as if we have exerted all our strength, and then a great letdown comes upon us. But God spoke to him again. Then in Genesis 15, we read how he doubted God's promise for a son. "And where is the promise You gave me for this land?" How gracious God was to Abraham until he believed.

Again and again, God built up Abraham's faith and He was able to give him the last test (see Genesis 22). God said, "Give me your beloved son; offer him to Me at Mt. Moriah." It took three days for Abraham to reach Mt. Moriah which was enough time for him to change his mind. But Abraham's faith had been built up through the years by God's grace and God knew he was ready. He knew that when He tested Abraham, he would come out even more glorious. And that is what testing is.

Abraham travelled with his son for three days. It gave him enough time to think it over before they reached Mt. Moriah. As he and his son ascended the mount, the son said, "Father, we have everything—the fire and the wood—but where is the sacrifice?" That spoke very deeply in Abraham's heart and he said, "God will provide." See that faith. He bound Isaac, he raised up the knife over his son, and God said, "That's enough." God has to try our faith; but remember, when He tries our faith, He has already put enough in us to pass the test. That makes our faith grow even stronger.

TEMPTATION COMES FROM THE ENEMY

There is another way that God allows to come into our lives to make our faith grow, and that is by temptation. We must remember that temptation never comes from God. God never tempts anyone nor can He be tempted by anything. It says in James that temptation comes from the enemy. The enemy tries to draw our flesh out because it is his ally. And when our flesh is drawn out, we lose our faith. But thank God, even though God allows the enemy to tempt us he cannot do anything to us without God's permission. How comforting that is! I will not say this is true of unbelievers, but so far as believers are concerned, once we are saved we are the Lord's, and the Lord will take care of us. He will never allow us to be tempted beyond what we are able to bear. Even when He does

15

allow us to be tempted, it is because there is something in us He wants to get rid of.

JOB'S TRIAL OF FAITH

The best example is Job who was not even an Israelite; yet he feared God. In his generation he was perfect, and God was able to use him to challenge Satan. Now do not be afraid. God will not use you to challenge Satan if He has not built in you enough faith to withstand. If it does come, it means by going through fire your faith becomes more precious.

One day God had His government and all His messengers standing before Him, and Satan also came. God challenged Satan: "Have you seen My servant Job?" Of course Job was Satan's target, so he told the Lord, "Is there not a good reason why he fears You? It is because You have surrounded him with a hedge. You have blessed him and given him prosperity; that is why he fears You. Suppose You take away all these things, and see if he will not rebel against You." What a challenge that is! But thank God, He knew. He had put enough faith in Job to know that Job could stand that temptation and when he came

16

through, he would be doubly blessed. God says, "All right, go ahead and do whatever you want with him but do not touch his life." You know how cruel Satan was. He took away everything Job had—not only his vast properties but even his seven sons and three daughters. That is what Satan is. But thank God, Job said, "God gives and God takes away; blessed be the Lord."

The temptation was not over yet. There was another day when God set His throne and the angels came before Him, and Satan was among them. God challenged him and said, "See My servant. I allowed you to attack him but see how he honored Me." Satan said, "Yes, everything he had was taken away but his life. You have still kept him strong and well. Suppose you attack his body and see what happens!" So the Lord said, "All right, go ahead; only keep his life." And you remember how Job was attacked in his body and he sat among the ashes scraping himself. But he still kept his faith in God.

THE FRUIT OF TESTING OR TEMPTATION IS SONSHIP

Job's three friends came to comfort him, but instead they hurt him. Nevertheless, in spite of everything, Job could say, "Even though He slay me, I will still trust in Him. But I know my Redeemer lives and someday I will stand before Him. I do not understand today, but someday He will justify me." And the Lord blessed him afterwards by giving him double of what he had lost. That is sonship. Out of his trouble and out of the attack of the enemy, he gained sonship.

This is what will happen to God's people. Whenever Satan tempts us, we must remember one thing: he cannot ever tempt us without God's permission. If we are being tempted, remember, it is because God has permitted it. Why does God permit it? It is because God knows there is something in our lives that still needs to be dealt with. Job's self-righteousness was something that needed to be dealt with. It was only through that temptation that Job came to the point that he was able to see that he was nothing, and he repented in dust and ashes. So

God accomplished His purpose wonderfully. His faith had been tempted by the enemy, but it only drew out what God had deposited in his life to make it more pure and more wonderful.

So if you are now under temptation, wondering why God allowed you to be tempted, remember that it is because He wants to purify you and bring your faith to such purity that you may gain sonship. That is what God will do with every one of us.

Before we enter into the subjective side of the triumph of faith or the consummation of faith, I hope first of all we understand what faith really is and know that our faith will be tested and even tempted. But God is behind it; He is in charge of everything and will bring us into sonship to the glory of God.

Let us pray:

Dear Lord, as we listen to Thy Word, we praise and thank Thee—how perfect is Thy Word! We thank Thee that Thou hast explained to us what faith is and also Thou hast shown us the way that faith will grow until we are conformed to the image of Thy beloved Son! Oh, dear Lord, how we praise and thank Thee that Thou art truly our heavenly Father. Thou loves us to such an extent that Thou will not allow us to remain as babes but Thou wants us to grow up into sonship. So Lord, bless Thy people, and may Thy Word make such an impression upon each one of us that we will give ourselves to Thee totally and faithfully, believing that Thou art perfecting us and bringing us into the fullness of Thy purpose. So Lord, we bow in worship. We ask in Thy precious name. Amen.

2. THE CONSUMMATION OF FAITH

Luke 18:1-8—And he spoke also a parable to them to the purport that they should always pray and not faint, saying, There was a judge in a city, not fearing God and not respecting man: and there was a widow in that city, and she came to him, saying, Avenge me of mine adverse party. And he would not for a time; but afterwards he said within himself, If even I fear not God and respect not man, at any rate because this widow annoys me I will avenge her, that she may not by perpetually coming completely harass me. And the Lord said, Hear what the unjust judge says. And shall not God at all avenge his elect, who cry to him day and night, and he bears long as to them? I say unto you that he will avenge them speedily. But when the Son of man comes, shall he indeed find faith on the earth?

I John 5:4-5—For all that has been begotten of God gets the victory over the world; and this is the victory which has gotten the victory over the world, our faith. Who is he that gets the victory over the world, but he that believes that Jesus is the Son of God?

Revelation 12:11—And **they** *have overcome him [Satan] by reason of the blood of the Lamb, and by reason of the word of their testimony, and have not loved their life even unto death.*

Let's have a word of prayer:

Thank You, Lord, for inviting us to Thy table. Thank You for reminding us what great love Thou hast poured out upon us! Lord, as we are touched by Thy love, we come to Thy presence and say, Speak to us, touch us, transform us, and make us ready for Thy return. We commit this time into Thy loving hand and trust that Thy Spirit will open up our understanding and bring us into Thy purpose, and it is all for Thy glory. We ask in Thy precious name. Amen.

As we have been sharing together on this matter of "live by faith," we come to this question: What is faith? Faith is the substantiating power that brings in the reality of

God to be our experience. Faith is not something that we look for within ourselves, for we cannot find it. Faith is like an anchor that has to be cast into God. The more we are conscious of Him, the more faith will rise in our heart. Thank God that He is the faithful One, and He always rewards those who seek after Him. That is what faith really is. But as we have mentioned before, in order for our faith to grow, God, in His wisdom, will test us to bring out what He has already planted in our hearts through which our faith is strengthened and increased. Or by His great wisdom He will allow the enemy to tempt us, and thus we realize how much He has already done in us to enable us to overcome temptation. Each time we overcome a temptation, it seems as if our faith in God gets stronger. This is our experience.

THE TRIUMPH OF FAITH

Now I would like to speak about the consummation of faith or the triumph of faith. In Luke 18 our Lord Jesus told us a parable about a widow who went to a judge to ask for justice. But it so happened that the judge was an unjust judge. He did not fear God nor did he respect man. So when that widow came to him asking for justice, he just ignored her. But the judge saw that the widow was very persistent. In spite of being denied many times, she continued to come and ask for justice. So finally the unjust judge said to himself, "Even if I do not fear God or respect man, she is annoying me. I have to get rid of her. Therefore, I will give her justice so she will not come back again." Our Lord Jesus used this contrast to show us that when we come to God, will He not answer our prayers surely and quickly? The Lord said, "Is there faith on earth at His coming?"

FAITH IN THE LORD GETS THE VICTORY

We have read in I John 5:4-5 that all who are begotten of God get the victory over the world and this is the victory that has overcome the world—our faith. In other words, there is a victory waiting for God's people. But how do we get that victory? By faith. Once we were under the power of darkness; we were hopeless and helpless. No matter how much we tried we were no match for the power of darkness. But thank

God, we find in Colossians 1 that He has translated us from the power of darkness into the kingdom of the Son of God's love. We are no longer under the power of darkness. On the contrary, we are under the kingdom of the Son of God's love. Victory is ours.

Why does the Bible say "faith is the victory"? It is not because there is something in faith itself, in believing itself. It is because of whom we believe. As soon as we are saved, we no longer belong to the world. We know that the world is something that Satan uses to control the soul of man. He uses the lust of the eyes, the lust of the flesh, and the pride of life to control people. This is Satan's tactic. But thank God, as soon as we believe in the Lord Jesus, we are no longer under that control. To put it another way, so far as the world is concerned, we are just strangers and sojourners; we are just passing through. This is not our home; we are looking for that city with foundations that God will build for us. And because of that, we are strangers and sojourners in the world. The world has no attraction for us, because we believe when our Lord Jesus came to this world, He was here as a stranger. He just passed through it; therefore, He suffered from the world. Even from the beginning of His ministry, He was tempted by Satan with the world. Satan said, "If you worship me, I will give You the whole world." And the Lord bid Satan: "Go!"

From the very first of His life to the very end, the world could not tempt Him. He said in John 12, "When I am lifted up, the prince of this world is cast out." When our Lord was on this earth, He overcame the world. That is the reason why faith is the victory because we believe in our victorious Lord. We cannot overcome the world because of our faith itself; we can overcome the world because our Lord has overcome. His overcoming becomes our overcoming. This is why the Bible says "faith is the victory." As we pass through this world, remember that so far as the world is concerned, we have been crucified; so far as we are concerned, the world has been crucified. We are the Lord's and we overcome the world. This is our victory.

A MAN OF SMALL FAITH IN A GREAT GOD

I remember when I was young and the Lord had saved me, I was so grateful to Him that I offered myself to serve Him. But even with that kind of desire, I served Him according to my will. What I thought He would like, I would do; but it was not according to God's will. Gradually the Lord began to open my understanding, and I began to realize if I wanted to serve Him it was not according to my will but according to His.

When I was in college, the Lord began to open my understanding. I began to see the will of God concerning His church. I was the son of a pastor in a Methodist church, and everybody expected me to succeed my father. However, the Lord began to show me that the church is the body of Christ—not an organization. Then the Lord began to bring a few others together who were seeing the same thing—just simply to remember the Lord, to seek the Lord and try to follow the Lord. We began with seven people— three brothers who were all classmates in the college and four sisters who were in a hospital on the other side of the city. One was the principal of the nursing school, one was the superintendent of nurses, one was a nurse, and one was a patient. The Lord began to show us the same thing. The first time we broke bread together in a sister's home, we all wept. The presence of the Lord was very real, and our hearts were so touched by Him. The Lord began to work, and all the nurses in the nursing school got saved except two. When God was doing such wonders in our midst, I was troubled by my own situation because I felt that I was standing on two boats, and the two boats began to sail apart. At that time, even though I was very young, it seems that the Lord had put the responsibility of His will upon my shoulder. I began to be troubled and said, "Lord, if I am standing on two boats—one the boat of denomination which is supposed to be my future, and the other boat standing on the will of God—and these boats are sailing apart, what shall I do?"

While I was in such perplexity, God sent a servant to us and he began to speak on Luke 14. He said, "A man who tries to build a tower should sit down and consider whether he will be able to finish it. If he is not able to finish it, then it is better not to start. Otherwise he will be laughed at by everybody." Or, "When a king is going to fight an enemy and he is only willing to use 10,000 soldiers against a king who comes with 20,000, it is better to make peace with his enemy before he starts a war." In other words, count your cost. As the brother was speaking, it touched me deeply.

After lunch there was a time of rest, and I was sitting in a chair praying: "Lord, why is it I cannot go straight? Is it because I have never counted my cost?" So I began to count my cost. But I discovered that if you try to count your cost, the cost will get higher and higher. I said to myself: "Maybe I will be discharged by the university. Maybe I will be driven out of my home. What shall I do?" I told the Lord that I could not do it; it was beyond me. Then I saw a vision in which I saw the Lord coming towards me, showing me His bleeding hands and He said, "I did all this for you, what will you do for Me?" What can we do? I told the Lord, "All right, I am willing to give up everything for You." But it was not that easy. Even though I had promised the Lord that I was willing, it took me three days and three nights of struggling with it. In the daytime I went to school, but I could not hear what the professors were saying. At night I could not sleep because I was struggling. But after three days and three nights, the love of Christ conquered me. So I finally told the Lord, "All right, I am willing to give up my future, everything to follow Thee." Thank God, He has kept me unto today.

It is not that I have great faith. No, I am a man of small faith, but I have a great God. He has sustained me ever since. Faith is the victory; and it is faith that one day will become sight. We have faith in God knowing that His purpose and His will for us is to conform us to the image of His beloved Son. One day, this shall be fact. One day our Lord Jesus will return and will receive us to Himself. What a glorious day that will be!

THE EARLY CHURCH

As I am thinking about the consummation of faith, I think of church history. In the first four chapters of the book of Acts we find that the church began on the day of Pentecost. What a glorious church it was when it first began! All those who believed persevered, continuing in the teaching and fellowship of the apostles, and in the breaking of bread and prayer.

THE TEACHING AND FELLOWSHIP OF THE APOSTLES

What is the teaching of the apostles? The teaching is in singular number and apostles are in plural number. The teaching of the apostles, whether it was Peter, James or John, was only one teaching. It is the teaching of Christ. That which they had received from the Lord, they passed on to us. The same is true with the fellowship of the apostles. Again, we find that the fellowship is singular in number. Peter did not have his fellowship nor did Paul have his fellowship. People would like to have made Peter or Paul their fellowship, but so far as the apostles were concerned, they had only one fellowship—their fellowship with the Lord. And what they received they passed on to us; therefore, we are all called into the fellowship of God's Son Jesus Christ (see I Corinthians 1:9). Their teaching is one, and their fellowship is one.

It is none other than the teaching of Christ and the fellowship of Christ in the Spirit.

THE EXPRESSION OF TEACHING AND FELLOWSHIP

In the early days, we find that the Christians, whether they had been following the Lord for two or three years or they had just believed and were newly saved, like the three thousand on the day of Pentecost, they all persevered together and continued in the teaching and fellowship of the apostles. How are we to express that fellowship and that teaching? By two things which are most prominent—the breaking of bread and prayers. If we look into the church today, we will discover that these two things are looked down upon. If we go to any of the great gatherings of God's people, we find that the two things most neglected are the breaking of bread and prayers. Often the breaking of bread is once a year, twice a year or once a month. But who thinks of breading the bread every Lord's day? It is too much. And so far as prayer is concerned, there may be several hundred people gathered together but at the prayer time, how many are there? These are the two things most neglected by God's people today; yet these are the two things that are most essential because they represent the teaching and the fellowship of Christ. How they persevered together! More people were added and everyone that was added persevered in the same way (see the first four chapters of Acts).

PROBLEMS IN THE CHURCH

When we come to the fifth and sixth chapters of the book of Acts, we find that there are problems in the church. No matter how perfect the church is, there is bound to be problems. We should not be afraid of problems because if they are handled correctly, there will be growth. For instance, there was a couple who tried to cheat the church. However, they were not cheating the church; they were cheating the Holy Spirit. Immediately the discipline of the Holy Spirit come upon them. When the church is in order, the working of the Holy Spirit is very prominent. Today, many things are being done wrong without any discipline; it is because of the low state of the church.

Another problem was the neglecting of the widows of the Hellenistic Jews. There were two kinds of Hebrews. One kind lived in the Promised Land, and the other group of Hebrews lived outside. There were differences between these two groups; therefore, there was bound to be problems. They solved the problem of the widows by appointing seven brothers to take care of it. The names of the seven people, except for one, indicate that probably they were Hellenistic Jews. They had no selfish ideas for themselves but only thought of their brethren. Because of this, the apostles were free to pray and preach, and God greatly blessed the early church.

PERSECUTION OF THE CHURCH

When the enemy saw that the church was handling its problems, he then tried to use persecution, which is always the case. He used Saul to persecute the church; but God brought Saul into His camp and he became the apostle Paul. In other words, we see how God works wonderfully in His church. Do not expect to have a perfect church, that there will be no problems of any kind. Wherever we are, there is bound to be problems. But thank God, if the Holy Spirit is there, the problems can be solved and the church will be blessed. That is what we find in the early days.

In the beginning the church was not persecuted by the Roman Empire because it considered the church as a sect of Judaism which was protected by the Roman government. The early persecution of the church came from the Jewish nation. But later on, when more Gentiles were added to the church and it began to grow, it could no longer be considered as only a Jewish sect. It was a different entity. When this happened, the Roman Empire began to persecute the church. During the second and third centuries, history tells us there was great persecution ten times from the Roman Empire upon the church. But even with all these persecutions, thank God, the God of glory used persecution from the enemy to purify His church.

We often see this in church history, that whenever there is persecution, the church is purified and faith begins to grow. Those who believe in the Lord mean business. It is human nature that when times are easy we begin to relax. During the two centuries of persecutions it was the Roman Empire that was defeated—not the church.

THE CHURCH WAS JOINED TO THE WORLD

Satan changed his tactic, for he knew that persecution could not destroy the church. So He tried to be a friend to the church. And you will recall that in 312 AD Constantine, a Roman general, was fighting to conquer the empire, and we are told that he dreamed a dream. In that dream he saw a flag saying: "In Christ conquer." We know that his army came mostly from Gaul and that most of them were Christians at the time when Constantine led his army to try to gain the Roman Empire. We do not know whether his believing in Christ was real or just a tactic to try to encourage his soldiers to fight for him. But he went forth under that flag and conquered the Roman Empire. If I remember right, in 316 AD Christianity was considered the state religion. Any soldier who agreed to be baptized would be rewarded with clothes and silver. And of course, to please the empire and to gain these benefits, who would not do it? Christianity became a state religion and Constantine ruled over the church. Many came into Christianity who were not saved. They did not know God, so how could they serve God? Needless to say, they could not. That is when the need to have people trained to serve God entered in, and this is the downfall of Christianity.

THE DARK AGES

From the sixth century to the sixteenth century AD, the church went into the Dark Ages. People did not even know how to be saved. They were taught that they had to accumulate merits in order to go to heaven. Only a very few people had enough merits to go straight to heaven when they died. Most of them did not. What were they to do? They had to go to purgatory when they died to be purged. So the teaching was that if you pray to the saints who had extra merits when they entered into heaven, they could share some of them with you and get you out of purgatory quicker; that is, if you paid a certain amount of money. You may laugh at this, but at that time it was very popular. Who did not want to go to heaven? If you just paid some money and it got you there earlier, who would not do it? Those who sold indulgences would tell the people that when the money entered into the box, the soul flew into heaven. Of course, if you had greater sins, you paid more. If somebody wanted to commit a sin, they could pay to get the indulgence and when they were caught, they could show the indulgence and they would be crimeless. Again, you may laugh at this, but it was very real. That is how they built St. Peter's cathedral. The way of salvation was not even known. It was certainly the Dark Ages. In other words, Satan seemed to succeed in his tactic. What he could not break with persecution, he broke with compromise.

THE RECOVERY OF THE TESTIMONY OF GOD

But thank God, in the sixteenth century, we often consider this time as the beginning of the recovery of the testimony of God. God raised up people such as Luther, Calvin, and others. They began to preach, and they emphasized two things. One was justification by faith. We are not justified by merits; we are justified by faith. That is the simple gospel, and it swept over the world. The second thing was an open Bible. The Bible, at that time, was not allowed to be read by the people. In monasteries the Bible was chained. But Martin Luther and the Reformers demanded to have an open Bible in the vernacular language or in the language where you lived. That was Reformation.

Reformation, of course, was just a beginning. From century to century after that, God has been doing the work of recovery. In the seventeenth century, the so-called teachings of mystery came in, and there were the mystics. They sought God and they found Him. In other words, they began to consider their spiritual life. Also, during that time God raised up the Moravians under Zinzendorf, and they began to go out spreading the gospel. God has continued His recovery work ever since. In the nineteenth century, God raised up the brethren who recovered the teaching of the church. Later on, in the twentieth century, God raised up one brother in India—Bakht

Singh, one in China—Watchman Nee, and one in England—T. Austin-Sparks. I believe God is still recovering His church. Go back to the original. As you come to the end, you go back to the beginning.

THE CALL TO OVERCOME

We know that at the end of the first century the Lord sent letters to the seven churches in Asia (see Revelation 1-3). All the apostles had died except John who had faithfully ministered to those churches in Asia Minor. Then he was exiled for the Word of God and the testimony of Jesus to the island of Patmos. On the Lord's day, he must have been looking across the Aegean Sea to the coast of Asia Minor. On a good day he could clearly see the coastline. As he was sitting there meditating about these churches that he had ministered to before he was exiled, he must have wondered what happened to them. Then he heard a voice. When he looked back, he saw a vision. There were seven golden lampstands and in the midst One like the Son of Man. And to every church the Spirit says to the churches, "He who overcomes."

We find that even during the first century, the call for overcomers had already come forth from God. He foresaw the downfall of the church; but His testimony will not fail. Therefore, to every church He calls for overcomers—those who overcome Satan the enemy, who overcome the world, who overcome their own selves and allow the will of God to be accomplished through them. Every century God calls for overcomers, and when the number of overcomers has been fulfilled, that will be the beginning of *parousia*, the presence of the Lord.

THE AGE OF THE KINGDOM WILL COME

Every century has its overcomers, but the number of overcomers has not yet been fulfilled. That is why the Lord has delayed His coming. We are on the verge of the change of the age—the age of grace will end and the age of the kingdom will come in. But who will be used by God to turn the age? The overcomers. Oh, how blessed it will be if one day or night suddenly all over the world some people disappear. Where did they go? They were taken to the throne. They are the welcoming party to the coming of Christ. They have overcome in their lives, and they are able to thrust through the air which is the headquarters of Satan and arrive at the throne, preparing our Lord to come to the air and then to the earth.

THE WAY OF OVERCOMING

The call to overcome is a call to all of God's people. But how can we overcome? Revelation 12:11 says, "They overcame the accuser by the blood of the Lamb." We can never outgrow the blood of our Lord Jesus. We need His blood every day. The closer we are to the Lord, the more we realize how we need the blood of Christ to cleanse us. The blood of Christ satisfies God's righteous demand. The blood of Christ cleanses our conscience. The blood of Christ shuts up the mouth of the accuser. The closer you get to the Lord, the more you need the blood. Somebody has said: "Even the tears of our repentance need the blood."

"They overcame by the word of their testimony." We are supposed to bear the testimony of Jesus. We are to show people who Jesus is—not only by our words but by our life. Is Christ our life? We are to testify to that. If we really live "not I but Christ," then when we say "Jesus is Lord," it is powerful. But if we do not live that life, even if we say it, it does not have power.

"They loved not their lives even unto death." That is their self-life. They are willing to lay down their self-life and allow the life of Christ to take charge over them.

These are the secrets of victory. As we come to the end of this age, the Lord expects us to be overcomers. We are not to be overcome by the world or ourselves, but to overcome by faith in our Lord Jesus. May the Lord make every one of us an overcomer! May that number of overcomers be fulfilled! That will hasten the return of the Lord.

Shall we pray:

Dear Lord, we say we long to see You come back, but we realize it is we who delay Thy return. So we come back to Thee with repentance, giving ourselves totally over to Thee, allowing Thee to transform us and conform us to Thy own image— not for ourselves but to speed up or hasten Thy return. Lord, have mercy upon us! Hear us, oh Lord! In Thy precious name Amen.

QUESTIONS AND ANSWERS

I always think "questions and answers" is not really a correct term because man can only answer something that is technical; only God can answer things that are real and spiritual. If you are hoping to get a right answer or a living one, man cannot give it to you. God alone is able and He is ready to answer our question if we seek Him. Therefore, all we can do is give you a little help and encourage you to go to God yourself. Whenever we have a question, the easiest way to solve it, as it were, is to go to someone and ask the question. But spiritually speaking, the real answer to all our questions can only come from God. If we do not seek the Lord ourselves, we may hear many people telling us what to do; but we are still outside the veil. It is not that we should not ask questions, but we should put our hope in our fellowship with the Lord instead of trying to depend on other people. The spiritual way is an inward way of life and not an outward way. Unfortunately, Christianity usually leads us into the outward way. It gives us some commands, rules and regulations, something we ought to do and not to do, but the only way for us to truly grow spiritually is for us to go to the Lord ourselves and seek Him.

Usually when we have the question and answer period, most of the questions are technical; but thank God, all the questions that we have received this time are practical not technical. I do see that it is a great improvement. It seems that all the questions are centered on one thing.

Q: Can you share how to enter into the reality of living continually by faith? Can you share something of your experience?

LIVING CONTINUALLY BY FAITH

A: It is the will of God that we should live continually by faith because the Christian life is a life of faith. But how can we continually live by faith? Oftentimes, when we encounter a problem our first reaction is: How shall I meet this situation? Usually, we will use our own strength, wisdom, or understanding. But thank God, He is teaching us. When we are using what is of our own, we cannot get through our problem. It is only when we cannot get through our problem that we will turn to God and look to Him, and that is the time He will teach us. We do thank God that He has not only saved us and cleansed us from all our sins, but more than that, we know that He lives in us. He is our life. But who is helping us to grow in Christ, to grow in spiritual life? Thank God, He also makes provision. That is why when we believe in the Lord Jesus, it is more than having our sins forgiven; that is negative. Positively, we find that Christ comes into our heart to dwell and becomes our life. More than that, God provides the Holy Spirit. As we believe in the Lord Jesus the Holy Spirit also comes to us and dwells in our spirit. The question is: What is the ministry of the Holy Spirit? The Lord has accomplished all the works of salvation. But who is showing us the way and helping us to grow in Christ Jesus that the life of Christ may grow within us? It is not by our own methods or efforts; it is by the indwelt Holy Spirit.

THE ANOINTING IS WITHIN

I John 2:27 tells us that we have the anointing, the unction, the Holy Spirit dwelling in us. He is responsible for us to grow and live and abide in Christ. The Holy Spirit will teach us in all things—big things and small things. Usually in big things we ask God, but in small things we do it ourselves. However, the Holy Spirit is the One who teaches us in all things, big and small. If we obey the teaching of the Holy Spirit, we are abiding in Christ. To put it another way, we will live within the veil.

As soon as we are saved the Holy Spirit begins to work in our lives. Therefore, we need to learn to be quiet before the Lord so that we can hear His still small voice. He does not come in the thunder; He comes in a still small voice. I believe every brother and sister have had such an experience. After we believe in the Lord Jesus, something happened. When we are talking, doing things or going somewhere, a still small voice begins to speak to us. If we are quiet, we will hear Him. Usually, what He speaks to us is against our personal, natural life. That is where the cross is working. That is where we learn to take up our cross, follow the voice of the Spirit of God, and let Him have his way. When we do that, Christ will increase within us. It is through the Holy Spirit that we really learn to live by faith or to live within the veil.

THE INWARD AND OUTWARD WORKING OF THE HOLY SPIRIT

When the Holy Spirit begins to work, it is in two ways—inward and outward. Inwardly, there is the revelation of the Holy Spirit. The Holy Spirit will reveal to us what is of God and what is not of God. Outwardly, we call it the discipline of the Holy Spirit which is not a Scriptural term; it is a practical term. The Holy Spirit will arrange our environment. I will not say that happens with an unbeliever; but for the believer everything that happens to us is not by chance. It is the Holy Spirit who arranges our environment—the people we meet and the things that happen to us. It is because He loves us so much. As the Bible says, "Even the hairs of our head have been numbered" (Luke 12:7). It is not only counted, but it is also numbered. So when you combed your hair this morning, number so and so hair fell down. That is the love of God. Through the circumstances that the Holy Spirit arranges, together with the revelation from within, is the way to enter into a life of faith or enter into the veil.

HUDSON TAYLOR

I would like to use the example of Hudson Taylor. He means a great deal to the Chinese because he was used by God to open up interior China. In the beginning, when the gospel came to China, it was in the trading places because they were protected by their government. But Hudson Taylor was the first one who penetrated into interior China, and he was the one who formed the China Inland Mission. He had been working in China for a few years; but personally and spiritually speaking, he was not satisfied. He found himself worrying about all the responsibilities he had, which of course is only natural. He did not feel that he had an overcoming life. He sought the Lord earnestly by reading the Bible, fasting and praying. As he was doing that, the thought came to him: If only I can abide in Christ, then I will be able to enter into rest. He struggled to abide in Christ, to get into Christ, until one day, the Holy Spirit opened his understanding. He was reading John 15 and the Holy Spirit reminded him: "You are trying to get into Me but I am the vine and you are the branches. You are already in Me. The branch does not need to ask to be connected to the vine; that is ridiculous. The branch is already in the vine and the vine is in the branch. Everything that is Christ is yours. Believe it." Hudson Taylor's whole life changed. Even in his old age, during the Boxer Rebellion, many missionaries, especially in the China Inland Mission, sacrificed their lives. Hudson Taylor was weak and sick, resting in Europe. When the news came, he found peace in his heart. So I think instead of using my own experience, I will use his experience to show us that if we listen to the still small voice and learn to cooperate with the Holy Spirit, we will be led into this life of faith. Or to put it another way, we will be living within the veil.

THE HOLY SPIRIT WORKS WITH INDIVIDUAL TEMPERAMENT

Christian experience seems to follow our temperament. We are made with different temperaments—some people are quick, some are slow, some are introspective and some are outgoing. Even though our temperaments are different, thank God that the Spirit of God seems to work with the temperament. We sometimes hear of people having a big experience that changed their whole life, and because of that we are looking for such an experience. But we must remember that people are different. Some people will go through big experiences in their life, while others will not, but they will gradually enter into spiritual experiences. And when you look back, you will find that you have already changed. So do not look for great experiences but look to the Lord. In His timing, He will bring you within the veil to live, and as you look back, you will see that something has happened.

Q: Is living by faith living in the presence of the Lord?

A: Yes, because faith looks to the Lord. As Hebrews says, "Look away, look off unto Jesus, the author and finisher of our faith (see 12:2).

Q: Is living in the presence of the Lord limited to the Holy of holies?

A: Yes it is the same thing.

THE CORPORATE ASPECTS OF "LIVE BY FAITH"

Q: Does "live by faith" have corporate aspects? If so, how do you enter into this reality?

A: Even though we are called separately, we are called into the one body of Christ. Therefore, we never stop at the personal level. We have to learn to be a member of the body of Christ. Whatever God may bring into your spiritual experience, He has no intention of making you a spiritual statue by yourself. Whatever experience He may give to you, it is not just for yourself; it is for the body of Christ. So we cannot separate ourselves from the body of Christ. Of course, so far as practical ways are concerned, I have known people who have gathered with God's people, but when they gather with other brothers and sisters, they find that not everyone is totally Christ-centered. Many are still living in the self-life with a little bit of Christ. If that is the case, there is bound to be problems. People will step on you and they may misunderstand you. So when you are with your brothers and sisters, you may think you are in paradise, but actually you are not. I believe that the place you suffer the most is the church. After suffering in the world and then you believe in the Lord Jesus, you are in the church. You may think you are in paradise and it is all rosy now, but do not be deceived. Life in the church is difficult. If it is all Christ, there is no problem, but our problem is there is more of self than of Christ. That is the reason why we find living in the body of Christ so close together is a difficult thing so far as the flesh is concerned. But it is a good training ground. God is using your brothers and sisters to purify you; therefore, whatever you learn in Christ, it is to be practiced in the church. Don't be disappointed when you are offended by your brothers and sisters. Continue with them, love them, forgive them and show Christ to them until you become a supply to the body of Christ. So that is the practice of entering into the reality of being one body in Christ.

ABRAHAM'S FAITH

Q: You remember that for Abraham, his faith grew over time despite taking his father and Lot with him. Can you share from your own experience how the Lord taught you in the matter of growth in faith? Can you also share what is the secret of becoming an overcomer?

A: I have to confess that my experience is very small; I am still learning. But thank God, He is faithful. We all make mistakes in the walk of faith, but mistakes should not hinder us. If we really have a heart for the Lord, the Lord will turn our mistakes into blessing. That is Abraham. He is called the father of faith but he had to grow in this because in the beginning he was not of faith completely. When God called him, he consulted with man and the result was that his father took the lead. And while he was at Haran, God was silent to him. But thank God, after his father died, God spoke to Abraham and he followed. At that time, he had to take Lot with him, and it was only by the grace of God that God separated Lot from him. So we see in the life of Abraham, the father of faith, how he grew in it. And as long as your heart is open to the Lord, as long as you are willing to confess your failures and allow the Holy Spirit to lead you and guide your steps, faith is something that grows. And gradually, you begin to understand the secret of an overcomer.

THE SECRET OF OVERCOMING

We find in Revelation 12:11 the secret of the overcomer. "The brethren overcame the enemy by the blood of the Lamb, by the word of their testimony, and they loved not their self-life even onto death" (see Revelation 12:11). That is the secret. It is the blood of the Lamb. You will never be able to outlive the blood. The closer you are to God, the more you need the blood of the Lamb because you see more of yourself. But the blood of the Lamb is always available.

Likewise is the word of our testimony. We have a testimony; it is the testimony of Jesus. We are here to testify Jesus before the world. If we really learn to live for Christ, the word of our testimony is powerful. You remember in the book of Acts, when Paul was in Ephesus, there was seven sons of the Jewish high priest Sceva. They were exorcists, and they used words to try to drive out evil forces. When they saw Paul was successful in exorcising these demons, they tried to use the same formula. They tried to drive out the demons by saying "in the name of Jesus that Paul preaches." We saw how the demons overcame two of them. In other words, it is really living your life in Christ, then when you speak the word, it is active. That is the word of our testimony. If you really live by Christ, when you use the name of the Lord, He will honor it.

"And you love not your soul-life even onto death." You are willing to take up your cross and follow the Lord. This is the secret to being an overcomer, and it is an open secret. You know it and if you practice it, then you overcome. May the Lord help each and every one of us. We are not perfect yet; we are all learning. Hopefully we will continue to learn until we see Him face to face. May God bless you!

Other Books Printed By
Christian Testimony Ministry

SPEAKER	TITLE
DANA CONGDON	MARRIAGE, SINGLENESS, AND THE WILL OF GOD
	RECOVERY & RESTORATION
	THE HOLY SPIRIT
	HEBREWS
A.J. FLACK	TENT OF HIS SPLENDOUR
STEPHEN KAUNG	ACTS
	BE YE THEREFORE PERFECT
	CALLED OUT UNTO CHRIST
	CALLED TO THE FELLOWSHIP OF GOD'S SON
	DIVINE LIFE AND ORDER
	FOR ME TO LIVE IS CHRIST
	GLORIOUS LIBERTY OF THE CHILDREN OF GOD
	GOD'S PURPOSE FOR THE FAMILY
	I WILL BUILD MY CHURCH
	MEDITATIONS ON THE KINGDOM
	RECOVERY
	SPIRITUAL EXERCISE
	SPIRITUAL LIFE (II CORINTHIANS SERIES)
	TEACH US TO PRAY
	THE CROSS
	THE FULNESS OF CHRIST—IN THE BOOK OF REVELATION
	THE HEADSHIP OF CHRIST
	THE KINGDOM AND THE CHURCH
	THE KINGDOM OF GOD
	THE LAST CALL TO THE CHURCHES, THE CALL TO OVERCOME
	THE LIFE OF OUR LORD JESUS
	THE LIFE OF THE CHURCH, THE BODY OF CHRIST
	THE LORD'S TABLE
	TWO GUIDEPOSTS FOR INHERITING THE KINGDOM
	VISION OF CHRIST (REVELATION)
	WHO ARE WE?

www.ingramcontent.com/pod-product-compliance
Lightning Source LLC
Chambersburg PA
CBHW060716030426
42337CB00017B/2894